D1682495

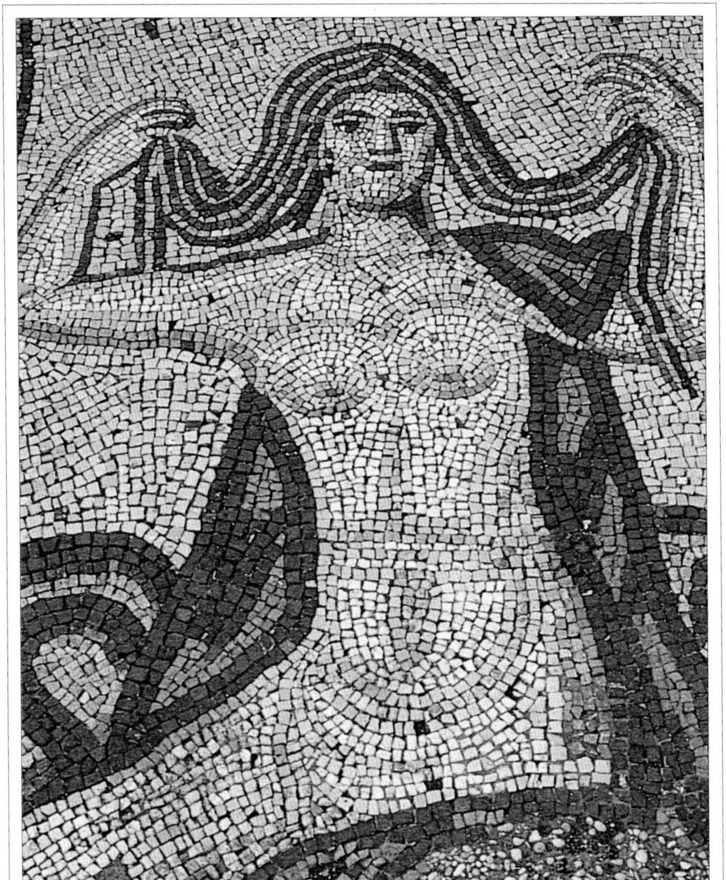

APHRODITE

GODDESS OF LOVE

Manuela Dunn Mascetti

GODDESS WISDOM

CHRONICLE BOOKS
SAN FRANCISCO

A Labyrinth Book

First published in the United States in 1996 by Chronicle Books.

Copyright © 1996 by Labyrinth Publishing (UK) Ltd.

Design by DW design.

All rights reserved. No part of this book may be reproduced without written permission from the Publisher.

The Little Wisdom Library–Aphrodite–Goddess of Love was produced by Labyrinth Publishing (UK) Ltd. Printed and bound in Hong Kong.

Library of Congress Cataloging-in-Publication Data: Aphrodite, Goddesses of Wisdom.

Dunn Mascetti, Manuela

Aphrodite—Goddess of Love by Manuela Dunn Mascetti.

p. cm.

Includes bibliographical references.

ISBN 0-8118-0918-8

1. Aphrodite (Greek deity) I. Title.

BL820. V5D86   1996
292.2' 114—dc20   95-8281
                                                    CIP

Distributed in Canada by Raincoast Books,
8680 Cambie Street, Vancouver, B.C. V6P 6M9

10 9 8 7 6 5 4 3 2 1

CHRONICLE BOOKS

275 FIFTH STREET, SAN FRANCISCO, CA 94103
CHRONICLE BOOKS ® IS REGISTERED IN THE U.S. PATENT AND TRADEMARK OFFICE.

CONTENTS

Introduction 9

The Myth 15

The Archetype 27

The Symbols 33

The Path to Wholeness 37

Fragmentation 45

Journeying Through the Archetype: 51

Step 1 - Unity and Multiplicity 52

Step 2 - Transformation and Development 54

Step 3 - Embracing the Goddess 55

Bibliography 59

Further Reading 60

Acknowledgments 61

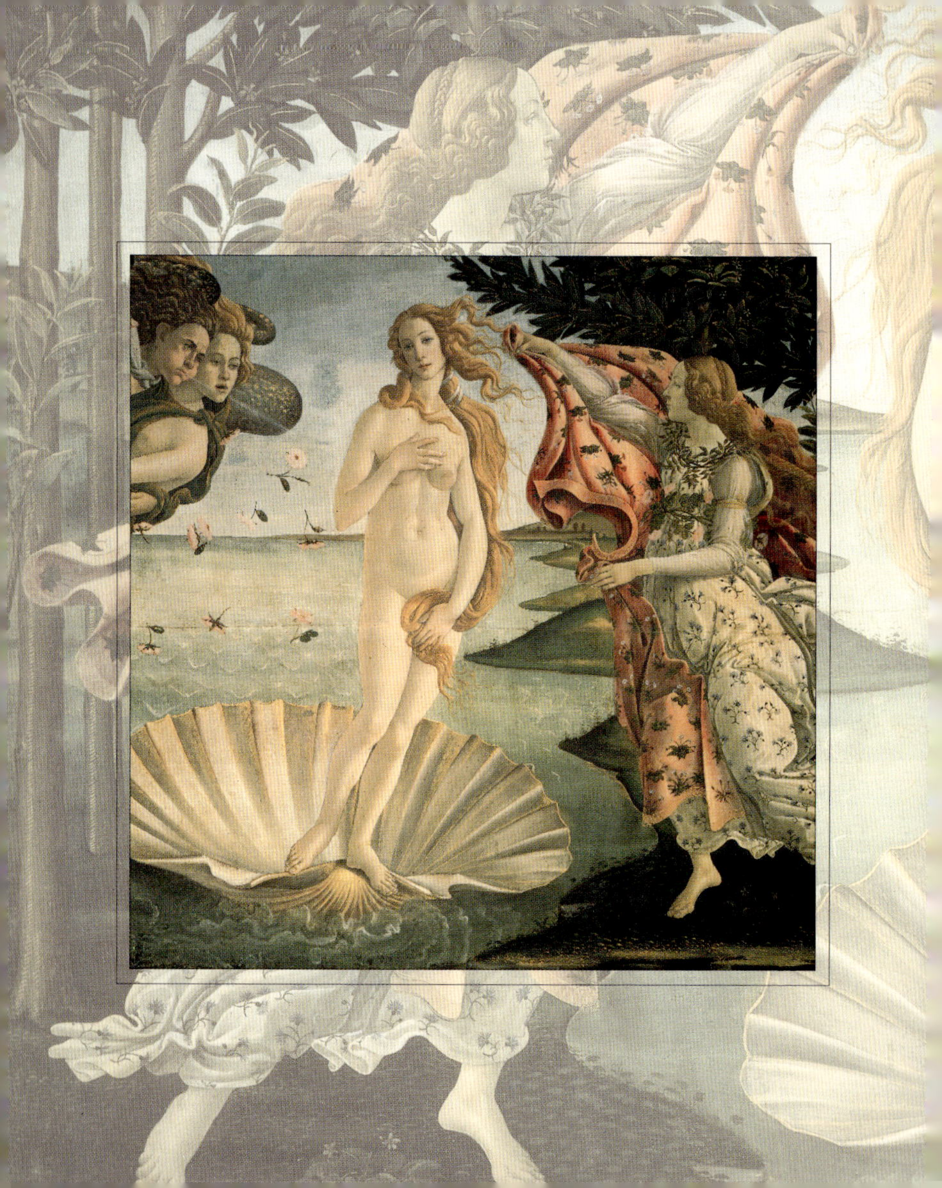

Introduction

APHRODITE — GODDESS OF LOVE

The ancient city of Paphos in Cyprus (now better known as Kuklia) occupied the summit of a hill to the west of the island. Although just a mile from the sea, Paphos was cut off from the rest of Cyprus by the Olympian Mountains, the abode of the Greek gods and goddesses. It was in Paphos that the goddess Aphrodite had her sanctuary, one of the most celebrated in the ancient world, where she was represented by a simple white cone, a symbol of fertility.

Aphrodite was worshipped as the goddess of love and fertility. She was the heir to a much older tradition, which had been manifested for centuries before by Ishtar and Astarte, goddesses of Babylon and Byblos in western Asia. In turn, Astarte and Ishtar embodied an even more ancient deity, the fertility goddess of the neolithic period, known as the Great Mother, an omnipotent female presence whose power was represented on earth by great temples, with many priestesses to serve her.

The Great Mother was widely worshipped. It was the custom for women to enter religious prostitution at her temple before they could marry and conceive. These harlot priestesses ensured fertility and bounty by binding their sexuality with that of the

INTRODUCTION

goddess; in her honor, they offered themselves as an immediate, physical manifestation of the goddess made flesh and taught the sacred ecstasy of sexual union, a form of spiritual training in many ways similar to the ancient tantric practices. The practice of temple prostitution gradually moved east to India via the island of Cyprus, where Aphrodite's major site of worship was located. India is probably the only country in the world where this particular offering to the goddess is still maintained today.

By the time the myth of Aphrodite had reached faraway Paphos in Hellenic Greece, much of the original power attributed to Ishtar and Astarte had been lost or diluted. The rites celebrated at Aphrodite's temple in Paphos were a distortion of the original ecstasy teachings— their orgiastic form led early Christians to believe that the entire population of the island of Cyprus was descended from demons.

APHRODITE — GODDESS OF LOVE

Tracing the goddess's ancient lineage, Jean Shinoda Bolen, in her acclaimed book *Goddesses in Everywoman,* has defined Aphrodite as the alchemical goddess: her power of magic and transformation makes her stand apart from all the other goddesses of Mount Olympus. Aphrodite is both independent like the virgin goddesses Athena and Artemis, and vulnerable like her more traditional divine counterparts Hera and Persephone. She promotes growth, change, and transformation in every relationship; and she inspires continuous development through attraction, union, gestation, and birth, compelling women to find fulfillment in both the creative and procreative process. The alchemy of Aphrodite centers on the transformative powers of love and beauty. The goddess was traditionally aided by Cupid, who shot arrows into human hearts to awaken them to love's delights. Aphrodite's extraordinary pale beauty has made her a muse to innumerable artists. She is the goddess of process and transformation. As a psychological force, Aphrodite helps us to develop, shift, and transform, constantly embracing the new.

Frontispiece: Detail of a third–century mosaic of Venus, from a house in Ostia.
Pages 8 and 9: The Birth of Venus, by Botticelli, *c.* 1482.
Page 10: In the circular picture Venus is seen consoling Love, one of her Cupids. *Page 11:* Courtesans offer flowers at the court of King Kassapa in sixth century Sri Lanka; it is believed that the orgiastic part of Aphrodite's cult had been imported from far away Asia into Greece.
Opposite: A Roman wall painting in a villa in Pompeii depicting Cupid, Venus, and Mars.

INTRODUCTION

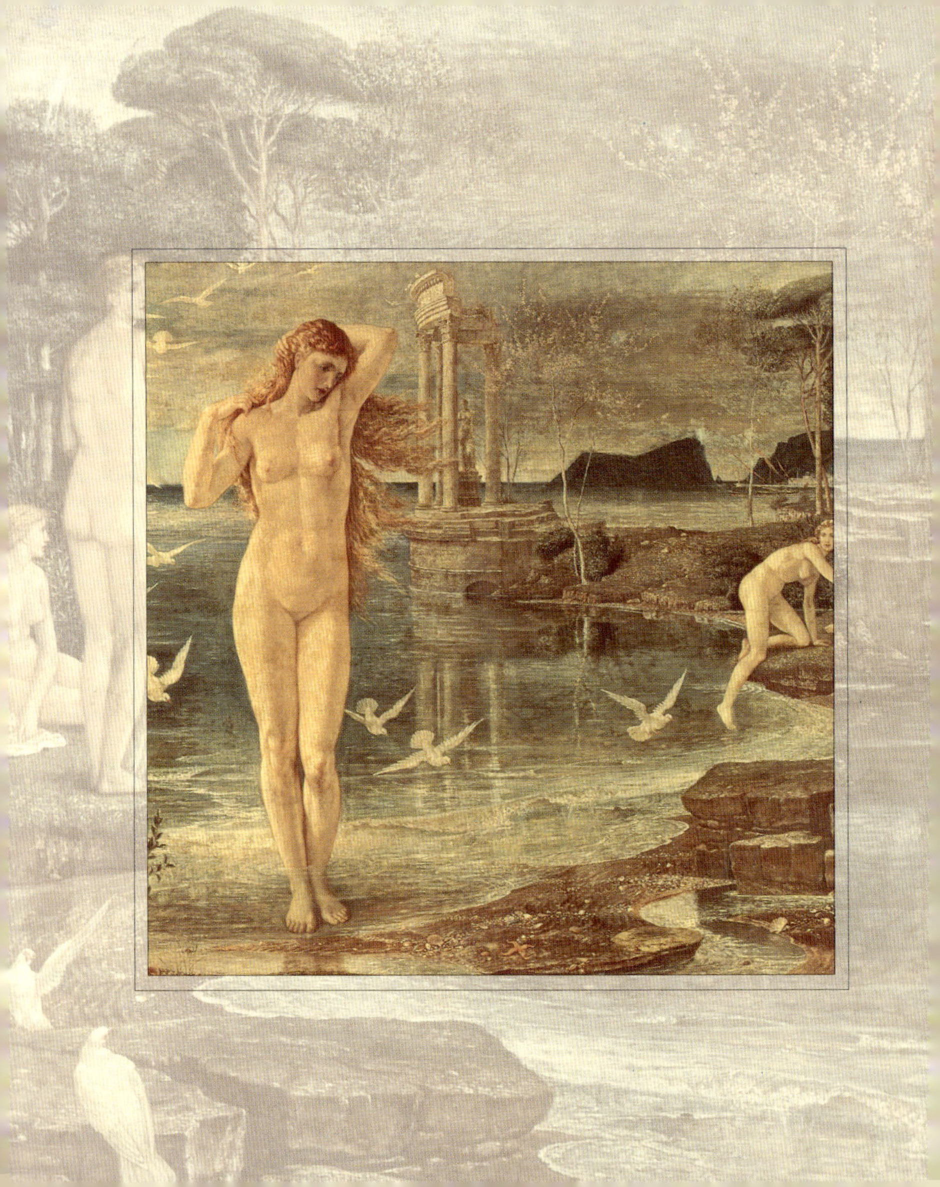

The Myth

APHRODITE — GODDESS OF LOVE

Aphrodite, known as Venus in Roman mythology, was very different from all the other goddesses of ancient Greece. She married and fell in love repeatedly but was never victimized, injured, or raped by male gods or mortals. This goddess always had the freedom of choice—she alone chose her island, her husband, and all her lovers. Love was for Aphrodite a path of learning, rather than an all-consuming and permanent bond that precluded other experiences.

According to the ancient Greeks, the world began from the union of Mother Earth and Uranus, from which the Titans were born. One of their children, Cronus (Time), resented his father staying with Mother Earth every night. He took a sickle (the crescent moon) from Mother Earth, castrated Uranus while he was sleeping, and threw his severed genitals into the Aegean Sea. The waters were thus made fertile, and it was from those waves that Aphrodite was born. In consequence, Aphrodite is often depicted as a sea-divinity: in one of her temples in Cythera, an island off the coast of Crete, Aphrodite is shown blowing a triton shell; the floors of her palace at Concise, the capital of Crete, were paved with seashells, and her altar was surrounded by sea anemones.

Previous pages: The renaissance of Venus by Walter Crane (1845–1915). *Opposite:* The depiction of a festival in honor of Venus; Flemish school of art (1600–1620).

THE MYTH

APHRODITE—GODDESS OF LOVE

The Birth of Aphrodite

Aphrodite, goddess of desire, rose naked from the foam of the sea and, riding on a scallop shell, stepped ashore first on the island of Cythera. But finding this only a small island, she passed on to the Peloponnese and eventually took up residence at Paphos, in Cyprus, still the principal seat of her worship. Grass and flowers sprang from the soil wherever she trod. At Paphos, the Seasons, daughters of Themis, hastened to clothe and adorn her.

Aphrodite's Deeds

Aphrodite possessed a magic girdle which made everyone who saw her fall under her spell. She chose to marry the lame Smith-god Hephaestus, but true to her myth and nature, she continued to love other gods and mortal men. Through her long relationship with Ares, the god of war, she conceived three children—Phobus, Demus, and Harmonia—whom she pretended had been fathered by Hephaestus. Hephaestus knew nothing of her

THE MYTH

deception until, one night, the two lovers lingered too long in their bed. They were discovered by the rising sun, who told Hephaestus. Hephaestus was enraged and set his heart on revenge. He crafted an invisible net with which he surrounded Aphrodite's bed, then announced that he had to go away. As soon as he had gone, Ares came to Aphrodite, and as they made passionate love, they became entangled in the net. Hephaestus soon returned home, and finding the lovers trapped in their bed, he summoned all the gods to witness his wife's shame.

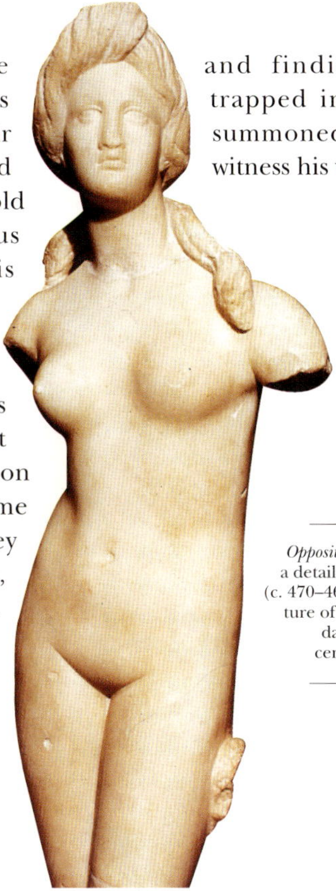

Opposite: The Birth of Aphrodite, a detail on the Ludovisi throne (c. 470–460 B.C.). *This page:* A sculpture of the goddess Aphrodite dating from the first century B.C. (Cyprus).

APHRODITE — GODDESS OF LOVE

In front of the assembled gods, Hephaestus demanded that Zeus, who had adopted Aphrodite as his daughter when she landed on Cythera, return him his wedding gifts. Zeus, angered by Hephaestus's public humiliation of Aphrodite, refused to comply. Poseidon (the god of the sea), seeing Aphrodite naked, promptly fell in love with her; Hermes (messenger of the gods) was also rapidly succumbing to Aphrodite's charms and claimed to envy Ares's position. Poseidon, however, was quicker. Hoping to win her favor by releasing her from the bond, Poseidon offered to ensure that Ares pay back an amount equivalent to the wedding gifts, which satisfied Hephaestus and set Aphrodite and Ares free.

THE MYTH

Above: A statue of sleeping Hermaphroditus, the love child of Aphrodite and Hermes, who was both male and female.

Wishing to put the whole unhappy episode behind her, Aphrodite returned to Paphos, where she renewed her virginity by bathing in the sea from which she had been born. She was, however, unable to forget Hermes's declaration of admiration for her. Overcome with desire, Aphrodite finally spent a night with Hermes and conceived a child whom she named Hermaphroditus, who was both male and female. But the story did not finish here: Aphrodite had not yet thanked Poseidon for his protective instincts towards her. She realized that she had fallen in love with him too, and eventually she bore him two strong sons, Rhodus and Herofilus.

APHRODITE — GODDESS OF LOVE

Aphrodite went on to have many other children by many mortal men as well: with Adonis she gave birth to a son, Golgos, and a daughter, Beroë; and with Butes the Argonaut, she conceived Eryx, who became King of Sicily. She also gave birth to Aeneas, whose story was recounted in the Aeneid. He was a major character in both Greek and Roman mythology. After the fall of Troy, Aeneas traveled far in search of a new fatherland. Eventually, he arrived on the banks of the Tiber river, where he married the daughter of the local king and became the founder to the whole Roman race.

Right: Female beauty comes in many forms, as shown in this figurine from Tell Selenkayiye.

THE MYTH

It was Aphrodite's love for Aeneas's father, Anchises, which led to a rift between her and her adoptive father, Zeus, which never fully healed. Zeus was a strong and lusty god, who was tempted constantly by Aphrodite's loveliness. He knew that, as Aphrodite's father, his feelings for her were inappropriate and could lead only to unhappiness.

Endlessly frustrated by the impossibility of the situation, he made her fall in love with a mortal, Anchises, hoping that by spending time with Anchises, Aphrodite would spend less time unwittingly tempting Zeus.

Aphrodite's desire for Anchises grew quickly. She soon became

Above: A beautiful nude by Alfred Chaney Johnston—Aphrodite symbolizes feminine beauty and mystery.

APHRODITE — GODDESS OF LOVE

obsessed with him and desperate for his love. She decided to visit him and seduce him, but afraid that he might be overly intimidated by the thought of loving a goddess, she disguised herself as a Phrygian princess. Her ruse was successful. Anchises succumbed and the two made love beneath the bearskins in his hut.

That night, Aphrodite dreamed that she and Anchises would have a son, Aeneas, who would one day be famous. When she woke at dawn, her disguise in disarray, she inadvertently revealed her true identity to Anchises. She made him promise never to tell anyone what had happened, but soon after, when drunk and unhappy, Anchises confided in one of his companions and was overheard by the ever-watchful Zeus. Jealous despite himself and enraged by the mortal's boasting, Zeus cast a fiery thunderbolt at the man—but he had forgotten about Aphrodite. Desperate to protect her lover, she deflected the thunderbolt and saved his life, but was never again so fond of Zeus.

Opposite: Venus in an act of seduction; this fresco adorns one of the walls of her temple in Pompeii.

THE MYTH

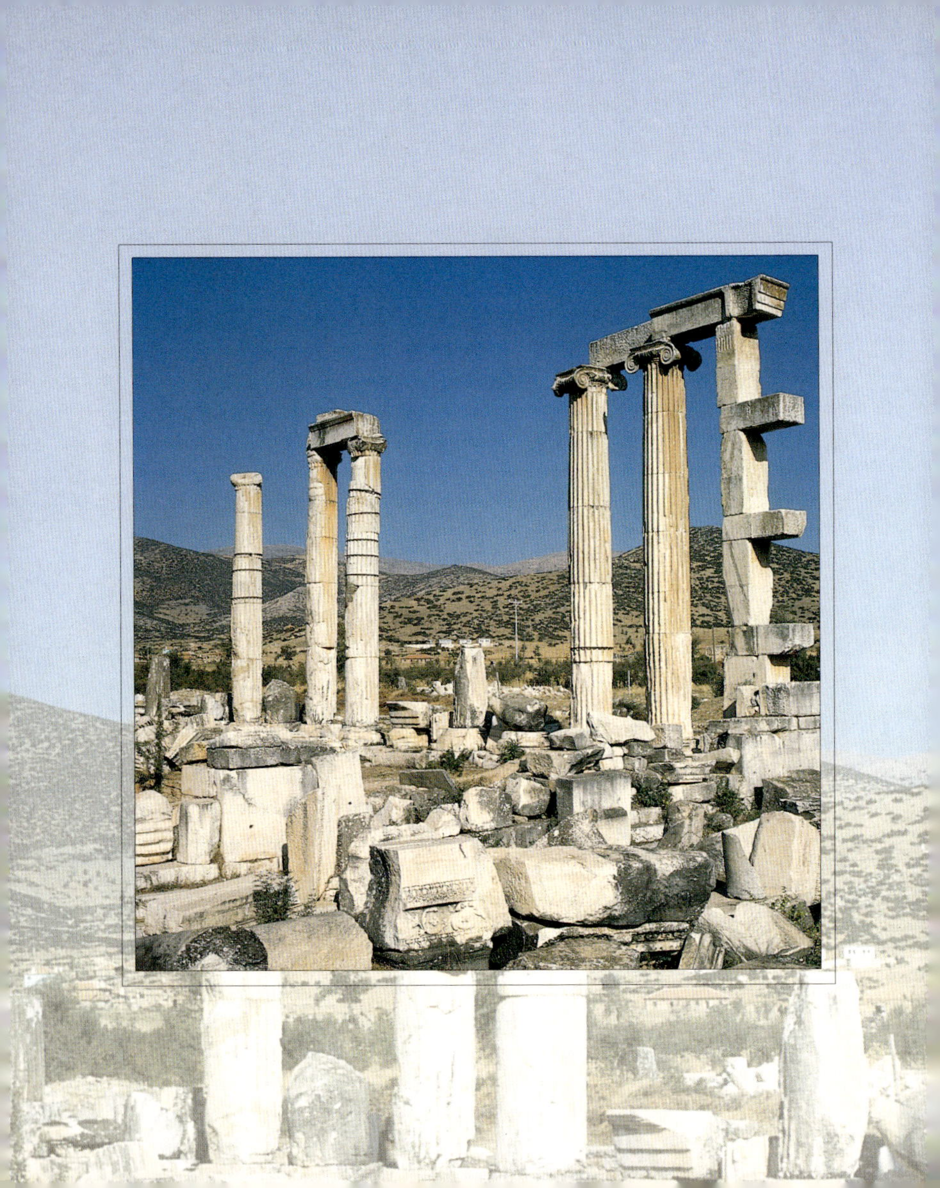

The Archetype

APHRODITE — GODDESS OF LOVE

The archetype of Aphrodite governs women's enjoyment of love and sensuality, beauty, and sexuality. The main expression of the archetype is as a lover: Aphrodite awakens within us when our body awakens to sensual and sexual perceptions; when we feel with every inch of our skin; when we feel pulsing circuits of energy running right through our bodies at the sight of someone we are attracted to.

Aphrodite energy makes a woman effortlessly, endlessly charismatic. She is engaging, attractive, and enjoys her unselfconscious sexuality to the fullest. She is surrounded by an aura of sensuality which works like the magic girdle in the myth, drawing others towards her and making them long to bask in the warmth of her charmed circle.

THE ARCHETYPE

Feelings, intensity, and variety are immensely important for Aphrodite. She becomes totally engrossed in her relationships, whether they are with a lover, or a friend, or even with a creative pursuit such as writing, music, dance, or therapy. Her ambitions tend towards the personal—the achievement of love is infinitely more important to her than the pursuit of power.

Aphrodite has been categorized as the alchemical goddess because she brings change to all her relationships: the object of her love is transformed and strengthened by her love and attention. This goddess promotes curiosity, generosity of the heart, undivided and focused attention.

Previous pages: First century B.C. Temple of Aphrodite at Aphrodisias, Turkey.
Above: The archetype of Aphrodite governs women's enjoyment of sensuality and sexuality. Shown here is the well-known painting by Jean-Auguste-Dominique Ingres, *The Grand Odalisque* (1814).

APHRODITE — GODDESS OF LOVE

When the Aphrodite archetype is active, a woman finds her deepest fulfillment in relationship and in creation. Dreaming, and making dreams come true, is a natural gift of Aphrodite and as a creator she is intensely interested in manifesting her own, and other people's, visions. In a creative community, of which she would most probably be the founding member, Aphrodite offers sanctuary where dreams can be realized.

The activation of the Aphrodite archetype can be dramatic and profound: sexual chemistry is often aroused unexpectedly, like Aphrodite arising from the waves of the Aegean Sea. Nothing warns us of what is about to happen, and we are often unaware of the journey we are embarking on until we are halfway there. We are simultaneously exhilarated and terrified. Our sexuality becomes instinctive, primal and raw, light years away from civilized, rational thought. It sometimes seems to be simply out of control.

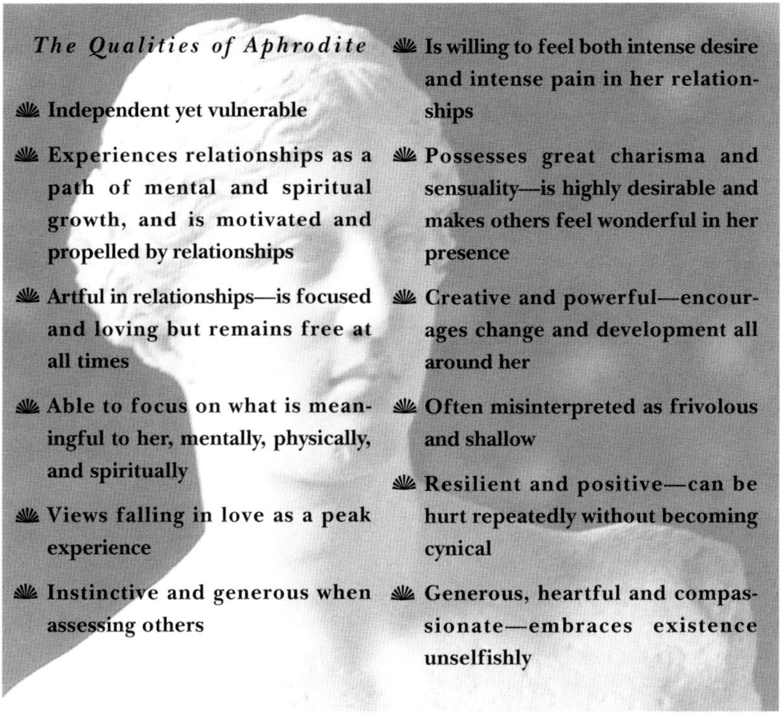

THE ARCHETYPE

The Qualities of Aphrodite

- Independent yet vulnerable

- Experiences relationships as a path of mental and spiritual growth, and is motivated and propelled by relationships

- Artful in relationships—is focused and loving but remains free at all times

- Able to focus on what is meaningful to her, mentally, physically, and spiritually

- Views falling in love as a peak experience

- Instinctive and generous when assessing others

- Is willing to feel both intense desire and intense pain in her relationships

- Possesses great charisma and sensuality—is highly desirable and makes others feel wonderful in her presence

- Creative and powerful—encourages change and development all around her

- Often misinterpreted as frivolous and shallow

- Resilient and positive—can be hurt repeatedly without becoming cynical

- Generous, heartful and compassionate—embraces existence unselfishly

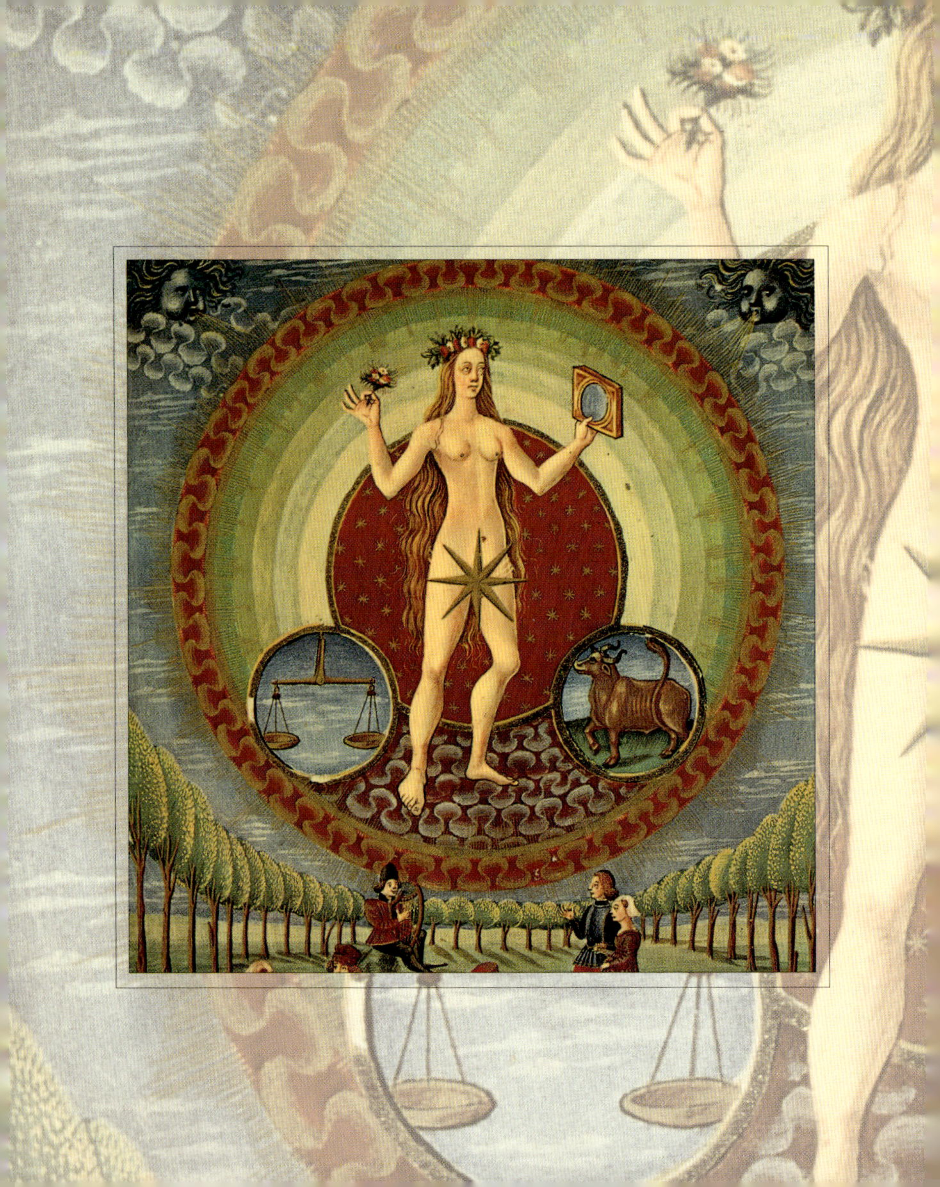

The Symbols

APHRODITE—GODDESS OF LOVE

The Symbols of the Goddess

The Magic Girdle

This is a symbol of the power of the womb, which longs to be filled with life. Women of African tribes still practice ritual scarification on the belly and stomach in rites of passage from childhood to puberty. The core of woman's femininity, her womb, is thus acknowledged to have undergone an expansion and magnification of power, transforming the girl into a woman and a cosmic being.

Previous pages: Love under the Influence of Venus, a fifteenth–century illustration from the De Sphaera *manuscript, housed in the Biblioteca Estense in Modena, Italy.* Opposite: The Renaissance of Venus, *a beautiful painting depicting the birth of the goddess by Walter Crane.*

The Sea

A symbol of inexhaustible vital energy and of the abyss which swallows everything. As a reservoir of countless sunken treasures, it represents the unconscious; as an immeasurably great surface, it is a symbol of infinity.

The White Cone

The white cone, which represented Aphrodite at her temple in Paphos, was often depicted as a circle on top of a triangle. This symbol was associated with all the great fertility goddesses: Astarte, Ishtar, and Aphrodite. The white cone represented the ascent and transformation of physical energy from sexuality to spirituality.

THE SYMBOLS

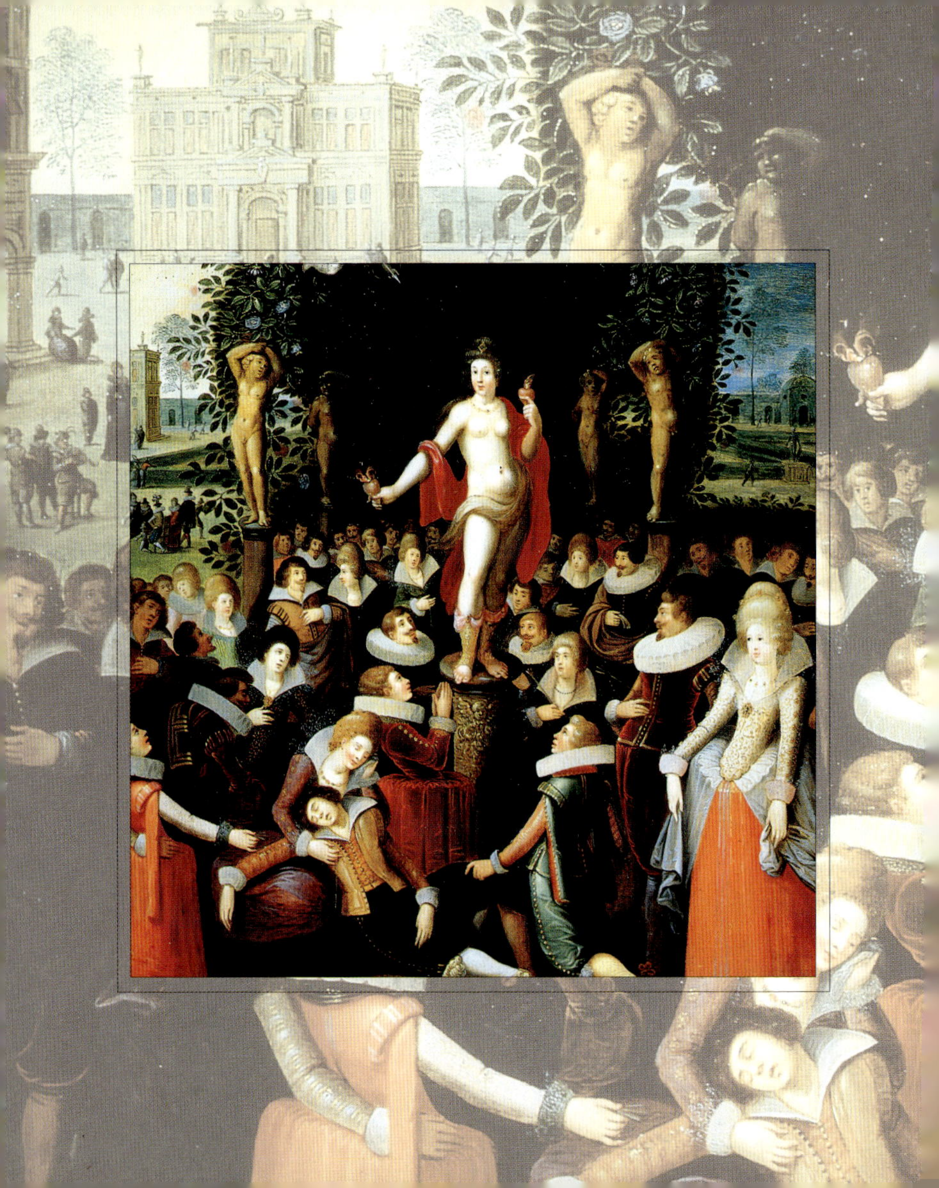

The Path to Wholeness

APHRODITE—GODDESS OF LOVE

Archetypes are innate energy fields rooted in our psyches. Apart from personal experiences, which are recorded within the *personal* unconscious, there is a range of inborn responses to life which are stored within the *collective* unconscious. Carl G. Jung was the first eminent doctor and scientist to individuate the existence of the collective unconscious, and he called its contents *archetypes*. One form of their conscious expression is found within the frame of mythology; other forms can be recognized as those universal trends which, although manifested in a myriad different forms, appear as psychic patterns in all of us. Archetypes represented by the goddesses are energy forces which did not originate within our personal consciousness, which can be recognized in our psyche as instinctive impulses which move and motivate us. They work like hidden magnets, exerting their subtle pull on us at all times, releasing explosive shots of energy at particular moments.

Aphrodite energy has multiple psychological and physical manifestations. The goddess demands an all-around expression. When gripped by this archetype and encountering life with the fullness of Aphrodite, a woman may feel as though she is undergoing a total transformation, finding passion and deep commitment in everything she does.

Opposite: Botticelli's *The Birth of Venus.*

THE PATH TO WHOLENESS

The Lover

Depicted by Botticelli in his famous painting *The Birth of Venus* as blonde and incredibly lovely, Aphrodite has always been seen as young and desirable. Similarly, when we fall in love, we feel "young" whatever our age; we feel beautiful, desired, desiring.

When we meet someone whom we find attractive, the Aphrodite energy buried deep within our soul begins to resonate and fire: this is when our stomach feels empty, our knees weak; our focus narrows suddenly onto one individual. The sudden rush of energy can feel so thrilling that there is a real danger of becoming addicted to the heightened feeling. This is the archetype being activated deep within in our psyche.

APHRODITE — GODDESS OF LOVE

Aphrodite as an archetype seems at first to be full of contradiction. She is independent yet vulnerable, in charge of her relationships but also driven by her heart, and extremely loving to all her partners despite her frequent unfaithfulness. With closer analysis it becomes clear that she represents a fine balance between the single-mindedness of Artemis and Athena and the vulnerability of other goddesses. She pursues emotional fulfillment, rather than worldly recognition and social achievement; she is courageous and strong when faced with conflict and aggression; and there is never any doubt that her lovers adore her and would choose to love her all over again.

The Alchemical Goddess

When the Aphrodite archetype is active in a woman's psyche, her consciousness is focused and receptive. She sees more clearly the true essence of a situation, concentrates her attention on her love and her lover, and is transformed in the process. Existence for Aphrodite is a never ending, ever changing process of creation. She falls in love constantly and repeatedly, not only with those who love her, but also with ideas, concepts, and places. Like the connoisseur of great wines, Aphrodite can appreciate all the positive qualities of someone or something, yet remain detached and objective. She uses both conscious, reasoned attitudes and

THE PATH TO WHOLENESS

unconscious, instinctual processes to further her knowledge: she takes in both the known and the hidden, and is able to decipher both. This type of consciousness, which is unique to Aphrodite, functions best in the creative process. Creation is the unveiling of the invisible, the discovery of the new, and Aphrodite encourages transformation in every relationship: ideas and concepts are nurtured, creativity is encouraged, and visions are supported until they become a firm and lasting reality.

Left: The famous sculpture of *Venus de Milo*, the Louvre Museum, Paris.

APHRODITE — GODDESS OF LOVE

The Creator

The true spirit of Aphrodite is a provider of love and passion, whose activation in the psyche causes dreams to come true.

There is an episode in Aphrodite's myth in which Pygmalion falls in love with his own sculpture of a beautiful woman named Galatea. He is tormented by his passion for the cold, stone beauty until the goddess comes to his aid. She brings the statue to life, and so allows Pygmalion and Galatea to explore their passion together. This story recalls and reinforces Aphrodite's powers of alchemical transformation: she has the capacity to transform everything she comes into contact with, whether objects or people, from the commonplace into the miraculous. The Aphrodite woman will exercise her power of love and transformation on those she loves: her family, her companion, and her children. She can be experienced as both creator and muse, and while she can bring her own miracles into fruition, she is also happy supporting those she loves, encouraging them to create their own joy. Her presence allows a true creative spirit to blossom and thrive in our lives.

Opposite page: Mars and Venus resting under a canopy held by cupids, painting by Poussin.

THE PATH TO WHOLENESS

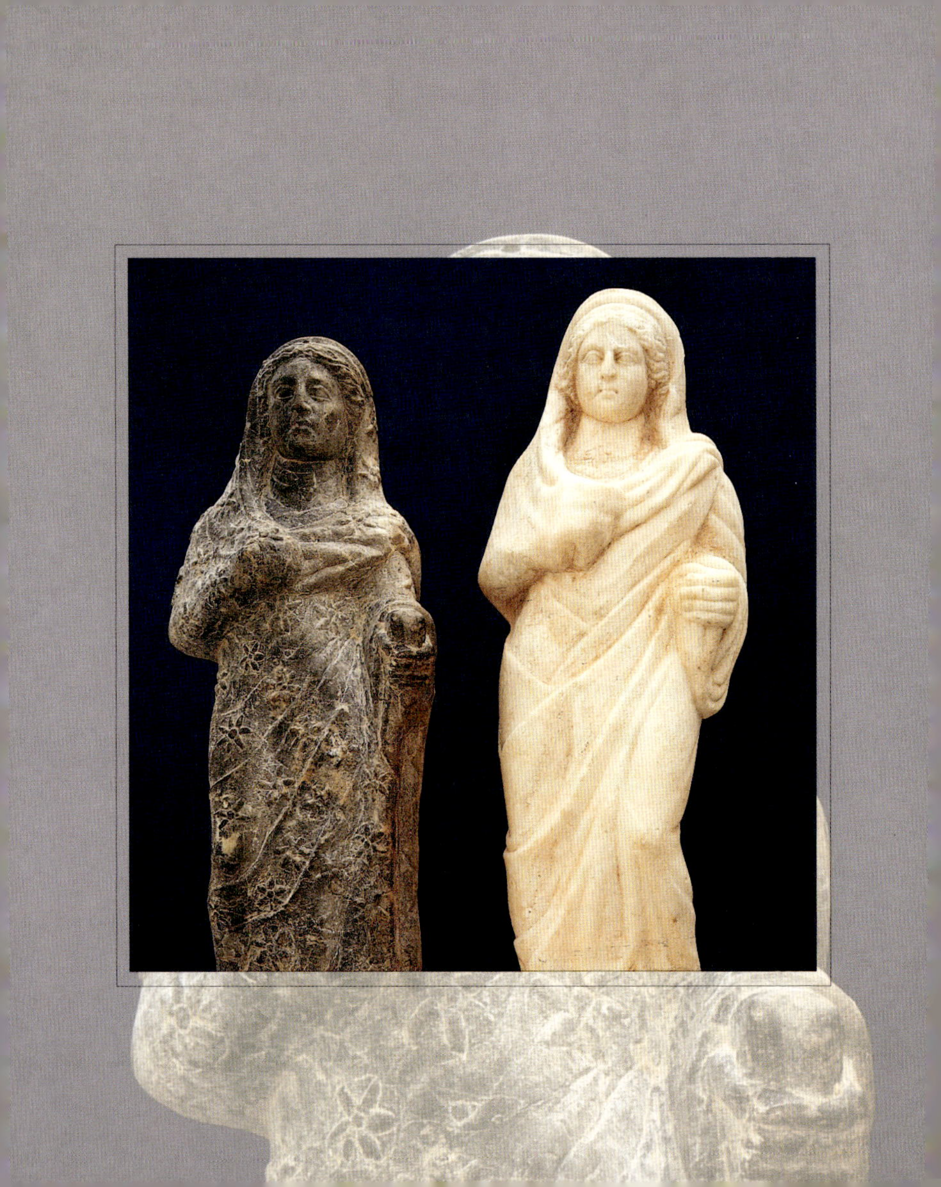

Fragmentation

APHRODITE — GODDESS OF LOVE

Aphrodite is an overwhelmingly forceful archetype which is difficult to control as the main moving force in our psyche: she demands such space and total surrender to her transformative powers. She is blessed and cursed with an unselfconscious sexuality, which she sees as a gift which should be enjoyed whenever and however it emerges.

In a sexually repressive environment, Aphrodite energy might be viewed with suspicion, or even denied. With her essential vitality and spontaneity repressed and condemned, a woman in whom this archetype is powerfully active is in danger of either lurching into promiscuity or withering into bitterness, distanced and distracted from the joyous sexuality and love which is her true nature.

Fragmentation also occurs when Aphrodite energy is misrouted, leading to a compulsive search for a love which is never fulfilled. This kind of search can occur after a short-lived love affair, a disappointment, or a long immersion in an unnourishing relationship.

FRAGMENTATION

In the relationships which follow, she might be reluctant to commit to an affair which she worries could develop into another stifling struggle for control; or she could feel a reluctance to open her heart to a lover who might mistreat or abandon her. She enjoys the thrill of new love but finds it difficult or impossible to commit to a more lasting relationship.

Having known extreme pain, denial, or disapproval, the woman being negatively influenced by Aphrodite may be drawn to relationships that bring her further conflict, humiliation, and pain. Aphrodite must learn to seek relationships which have a stabilizing effect on her psyche and to balance her sexuality with the

APHRODITE — GODDESS OF LOVE

learning inherent in all relationships. Once she begins to look for rapports that are positive, fulfilling, and truly sustaining with people who can give and receive love whilst remaining open and unafraid, then Aphrodite will be able to fulfill her mandate of love to the fullest.

Previous pages, 44–45: A black and white twin statue of Aphrodite, found in her temple at Paphos in Cyprus. *Page 46:* A detail of a wall fresco depicting Mars and Venus in her temple at Pompeii, Italy. *Page 47:* Gold statuette of Venus found in Cuzco, Peru. *Right: The Kiss* by Gustav Klimt—Aphrodite energy promotes the deep merging between lovers.

FRAGMENTATION

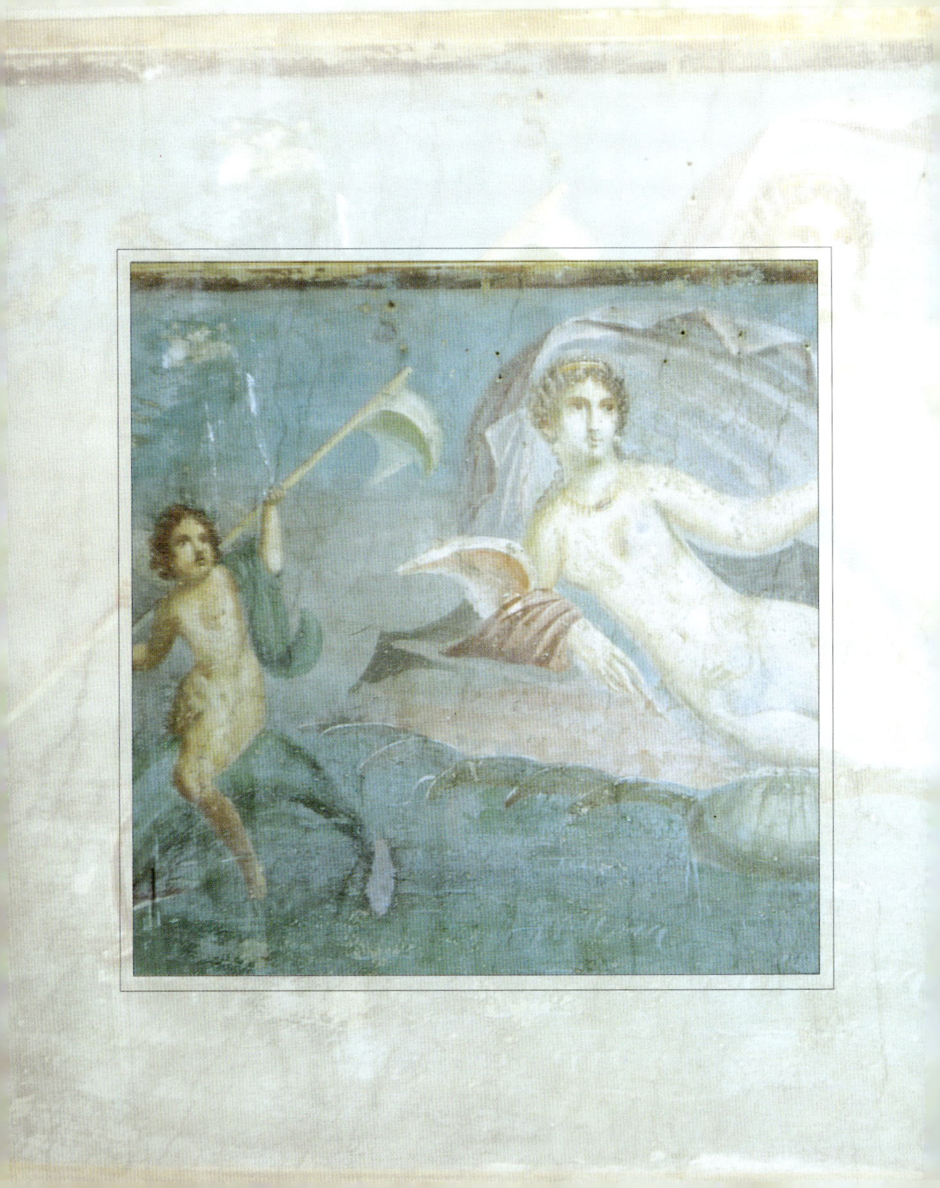

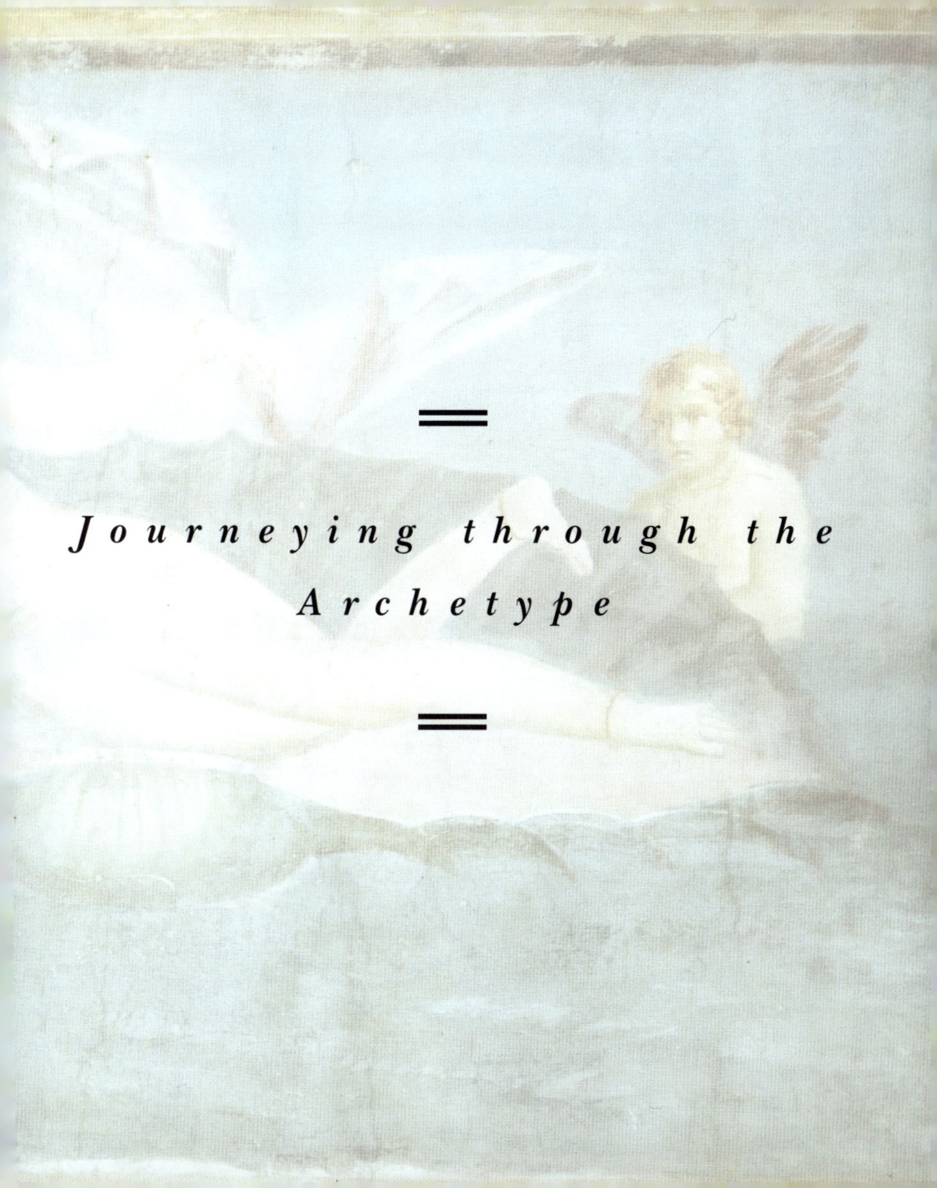

Journeying through the Archetype

APHRODITE—GODDESS OF LOVE

Step 1

Unity and Multiplicity

On a physical level, the Aphrodite archetype brings new life through the union of man and woman. On a creative level, it manifests and gives life to a new idea or creation.

Cultivating Aphrodite within us means learning to accept and strengthen our sensory and sexual perceptions, and focusing our attention on the here and now. Once we embrace our own sexuality and live each moment fully, the Aphrodite within us will bring about a complete change in our perception and flood fulfillment and joy into each moment of our lives.

Embracing Aphrodite involves the arousal of passion for someone or something. The creative process can be a very sensual experience for many women; taste, smell, touch, imagery, and movement can all be involved. Sometimes the whole body-mind-soul system is deeply engaged when giving birth to a dream. In the same way as the goddess fell in love repeatedly, so the archetype makes a woman process oriented rather than goal oriented, that is, finding attraction and fulfillment in variety. As one project ends, another arises, and another and yet another, transforming life into a constant creative flow of incubation and birth.

JOURNEYING THROUGH THE ARCHETYPE

On a deeper, personal level, Aphrodite also honors the rituals of femininity. In ancient times, menstruation, deflowering, birth and menopause-the Blood Mysteries of woman-were the four turning points of a woman's fertility which, at the height of the age of the goddess, were linked to the fertility of the earth and honored as an expression of each woman's divinity. In the past, these important moments were not dismissed as mere physical changes, as they are today. Instead, they were marked by rituals and initiations which celebrated their significance.

Previous pages: Venus on a sea shell: mural in the House of the Marine Venus, Pompeii, before A.D. 79.
Left: Aphrodite consciousness honors the rituals of femininity. In the past priestesses held the function of tending those sacred mysteries.

APHRODITE—GODDESS OF LOVE

Through reawakening the archetype of Aphrodite within us, we can recover those ancient mysteries and incorporate them into our modern lives. It is an initiation that forges an eternal link between each and every woman and the mystery and wonder of life.

brings fertility and abundance to all women who are touched by her. And whether experienced on a purely physical level or on a psychic, metaphorical level, her energy pours forth love and new life.

Step 2

Transformation and Development

Aphrodite is the goddess of process and transformation; her archetype is connected with sexual passion and instinct, with birth, and with beauty. Allowing Aphrodite to emerge in our psyche acknowledges that the creative flow of life itself exists within us. Aphrodite

JOURNEYING THROUGH THE ARCHETYPE

Step 3

Embracing the Goddess

When we can call upon Aphrodite to bless our sexuality, sexual love becomes a sacred communion—egos melt, time stops, woman and goddess are one. While such moments may sometimes just descend like an unexpected blessing, it is also possible to create them through ritual, awareness, and love; by listening attentively to the mystical workings of the goddess within.

Opposite page: The famous Paleolithic statuette of the *Venus of Willendorf*; primitive man recognized and worshipped the sacred mysteries of Aphrodite consciousness. *This page:* Aphrodite bathing; this Greek marble is called *The Venus of Rhodes.*

APHRODITE — GODDESS OF LOVE

The goddess is fluent in the languages of the soul and the body; she speaks to us through poetry, in our dreams and feelings. Embracing the goddess means speaking all her languages in order to tap into the wisdom that exists at our center. This wisdom sustains us in our soul-chosen path and, if we allow it to, will make every moment of our lives unique. It will transform life into an endless source of inspiration, hope, and joy.

This page: A painted marble depicting Venus found at her temple in Pompeii, Italy. *Opposite page: Venus in Vulcan's Forge* by Giorgio Vasari (1511–1574), Florence, Uffizi Gallery.

JOURNEYING THROUGH THE ARCHETYPE

APHRODITE — GODDESS OF LOVE

BIBLIOGRAPHY

Bolen, J. Shinoda. *Goddesses in Everywoman.* New York and San Francisco: Harper & Row Publishers, 1984.

Bolen, J. Shinoda. *Crossing to Avalon.* San Francisco: HarperSanFrancisco, 1994.

Graves, R. *The Greek Myths.* London: Penguin Books, 1992.

Jung, C. G. *Man and His Symbols.* London: Aldous Books, 1964.

Neumann, E. *The Great Mother.* New York: Bollingen Foundation, Princeton University Press, 1963.

Walker, B. *The Woman's Encyclopedia of Myths and Secrets.* San Francisco: HarperSanFrancisco, 1991.

FURTHER READING

Estés, C. Pinkola. *Women Who Run with the Wolves.* New York: Ballantine Books, 1992.

Harding, E. M. *Woman's Mysteries.* New York and San Francisco: Harper & Row, 1971

Perera, S. Brinton. *Descent to the Goddess—A Way of Initiation for Women.* Toronto: Inner City Books, 1981.

Woodman, M. *Leaving My Father's House—A Journey to Conscious Femininity.* London: Ebury Press, 1993.

ACKNOWLEDGMENTS

Picture Acknowledgments

AKG London, pages: 7—*Cupid and Psyche,* by Canova; 8; 25; 28; 39; 49.

C M Dixon Photo Resources, pages: 4; 13; 18; 19; 20—Roman replica; 41; 46; 50; 54; 55.

E T Archive, pages: 11; 14; 17; 22; 26; 32; 35; 36; 47; 53—*The Golden Stairs,* by Edward Burn-Jones; 56; 57.

Sonia Halliday Photographs, page: 44.

Range Pictures Ltd., pages: 10—*Venus Consoling Love,* by Boucher; 23; 30—Landscape, by Georgia OíKeefe; 43.

Text Acknowledgments

The quotes that appear in this book are taken from The *Greek Myths* by Robert Graves (published by Penguin Books, 1992), reprinted here by kind permission of Carcanet Press Limited.